Back and
Front

Jane Katirgis

Enslow Elementary
an imprint of

Enslow Publishers, Inc.
40 Industrial Road
Box 398
Berkeley Heights, NJ 07922
USA

http://www.enslow.com

Enslow Elementary, an imprint of Enslow Publishers, Inc.

Enslow Elementary® is a registered trademark of Enslow Publishers, Inc.

Library of Congress Cataloging-in-Publication Data

Katirgis, Jane.
  Back and front / Jane Katirgis.
    p. cm. — (All about opposites)
  Includes index.
  Summary: "Introduces the concept of the back and front, using repetition of words and short,
    simple phrases"—Provided by publisher.
  ISBN 978-0-7660-3916-2
  1. English language—Synonyms and antonyms—Juvenile literature. 2. Facades—Juvenile
  literature. 3. Polarity—Juvenile literature. I. Title.
  PE1591.K29 2012
  428.1—dc22

                                    2011007885

Paperback ISBN 978-1-59845-259-4

Printed in the United States of America

052011 Lake Book Manufacturing, Inc., Melrose Park, IL

10 9 8 7 6 5 4 3 2 1

To Our Readers: We have done our best to make sure all Internet Addresses in this book were active
and appropriate when we went to press. However, the author and the publisher have no control over and
assume no liability for the material available on those Internet sites or on other Web sites they may link
to. Any comments or suggestions can be sent by e-mail to comments@enslow.com or to the address on
the back cover.

🔁 Enslow Publishers, Inc., is committed to printing our books on recycled paper. The paper in every
book contains 10% to 30% post-consumer waste (PCW). The cover board on the outside of each book
contains 100% PCW. Our goal is to do our part to help young people and the environment too!

Photo Credits: Shutterstock.com

Cover Photo: Shutterstock.com

Note to Parents and Teachers

Help pre-readers get a jumpstart on reading. These simple texts introduce new concepts
with repetition of words and short simple phrases. Photos and illustrations fill the pages
with color and effectively enhance the text. Free Educator Guides are available for this
series at www.enslow.com. Search for the *All About Opposites* series name.

Contents

Words to Know

back   front

back

front

back

front

back

front

back

front

back

front

23

Read More

MacDonald, Suse. *Circus Opposites.* New York: Little Simon/ Simon & Schuster, 2010.

Yolen, Jane. *How Do Dinosaurs Go Up and Down?* New York: Cartwheel Books, 2011.

Web Sites

Hopposites
<http://pbskids.org/lions/games/hopposites.html>

Opposites at Enchanted Learning
<http://www.enchantedlearning.com/themes/opposites.shtml>

Index

Guided Reading Level: A
Guided Reading Leveling System is based on the guidelines recommended by Fountas and Pinnell.

Word Count: 10